Educatior

Paula Gomes

Educational Practices for Autistic People

Drawing up a Care Plan Using Psychomotricity as a Teaching Tool

ScienciaScripts

This book is a translation from the original published under ISBN 978-613-9-60762-4.

Publisher:
Sciencia Scripts
is a trademark of
Dodo Books Indian Ocean Ltd. and OmniScriptum S.R.L publishing group

120 High Road, East Finchley, London, N2 9ED, United Kingdom
Str. Armeneasca 28/1, office 1, Chisinau MD-2012, Republic of Moldova, Europe

ISBN: 978-620-7-30107-2

CONTENTS

SUMMARY

The aim of this work is to draw up a specialised educational care plan as a teaching practice, through the study of psychomotricity, specifically visuoperceptive skills. In this way, we hope to develop visuoperceptive psychomotor skills in students with autism spectrum disorder, as a resource for learning. We used bibliographical research as a source to develop the activities proposed here in the plan. We relied on references from the specialisation in AEE at the Federal University of the Semi-Arid, prepared for this course, books and articles whose subject matter was close to the proposed study. Among the authors are Bedaque (2015), Falkenbach (2010), Surian (2010), Freire (1996), the Department of Special Education and, as a highlight, Fonseca (2008), whose central theme is psychomotricity and the development of learning. The model plan proposed by Bedaque (2015) was used, adapting it to the research proposal regarding psychomotor activities. The results of this elaboration were described in ten activities, covering the five visual perceptual capacities, which are Fonseca (2008):" Spatial relations; background figure; visual motor coordination; consistency of form and position in space. We hope that from this care plan we have contributed to a playful educational practice, organised as a routine, to stimulate learning and arouse the interest of the student with autism spectrum disorder, in order to favour teaching with the teachers of the specialised educational care room, the regular classroom and contribute to the implementation of a school inclusion policy whose main interest is in developing in the student with special educational needs the desire to remain in the school environment on a daily basis based on new educational practices.

Keywords: **CARE** PLAN; AUTISTIC SPECTRUM DISORDER PSYCHOMOTRICITY.

CHAPTER 1

INTRODUCTION

This work was conceived from the perspective of building an educational care plan that takes into account the learning of students with autism spectrum disorder, more specifically their perceptual-visual abilities (psychomotricity). We know that autism, according to Surian (2010, p.10) is a "neuropsychological developmental disorder that manifests itself through marked and persistent difficulties in social interaction, communication and the repertoire of interests and activities". Based on this concept, we are using psychomotricity to provide students with a strategy to hold their attention and encourage the construction of a routine during the sessions that take place in the Specialised Educational Care rooms, using visuoperceptive activities. We have been thinking about this work since the beginning of this specialisation, because I work with autism spectrum disorder and a routine developed from psychomotricity could provide students with a good development in learning-oriented activities. We formulated this study based on bibliographical and documentary research, and by observing the school setting in which we work, hoping to favour learning in children with autism by developing a care plan focused on the student's visual perceptual abilities, during part of the weekly care sessions they attend. Visual perceptual activities can arouse greater interest in the child with autism in carrying out the activity, since these students generally interact with objects or remain fixated on an object more easily than they interact with people. Through the elaboration proposed here, ESA teachers will be able to apply it with the student and develop yet another means of teaching as an educational practice, both with autistic children and with the other students who take part in the activities in the classroom. Among the teaching strategies, we are thinking of organising a space to encourage this educational practice in the Specialised Educational Assistance room.

According to Freire (1999, p. 45) "The important thing is not to stop at

3

the level of institutions, but to subject them to the methodically rigorous analysis of our epistemological curiosity". We therefore sought to investigate in our construction, activities that would favour a playful educational practice, whose reality is established from activities that are creatively elaborated which aim to develop the interest of the child during their practice and in a pleasurable way reach the interest of the autistic student, transforming the school environment with activities involving play. For some authors, games and play are the same thing, but let's note that for Freire (1997) "play contains rules, while play has an uncompromising" random character and is carried out according to the need to satisfy the pleasure of manipulating objects and interacting with the child's imaginary or real thoughts. We see in play a possibility, together with psychomotricity, to attract the attention of children with autism, since the pleasure of manipulating objects is present, as well as the game being able to solicit a demand for interaction, or at least integration between the student with autism and their classmates, and associated with the playful way of playing, making it possible for them to socialise.

CHAPTER 2

PLAY IN CHILDREN'S COGNITIVE DEVELOPMENT: POSSIBILITIES FOR TEACHING

We will analyse the classifications of play according to Piaget. It can be seen that each stage of child development (sensorimotor, preoperative, concrete operative, formal operative) is characterised by a certain type of game that will be delimited by this work in order to better activate the child's cognitive capacities at each age. This does not restrict us to applying them only at a certain stage, since these games will be distributed according to each child's ability to play them, because as Braga Júnior; Belchior; Santos (2015, p.13) tells us, we know that:

> Global development disorders are characterised by: a severe and global impairment in several areas of development; social interaction skills, communication skills or stereotyped behaviour, interests in activities.

In this way, we won't be able to stick to the precise phases cited by Piaget as being exact in the autistic development process, but this study is looking for possible organisations to better develop activities with these children within the school process, respecting the construction of each individual as a subject.

Among the classifications, let's start with the exercise game (0 to 2 years), which is most often played in the sensory motor phase, as it is very much determined by the repetitive execution of motor gestures so that the child can accommodate new experiences to their motor repertoire. We can add that throughout most of their lives children acquire new motor repertoires, which means that this phase is not only extended to the first few years of birth.

In the pre-operational phase (02 to 07 years), symbolic play is very important as the child takes charge of make-believe. At this stage, the child tends to play imitation games with great pleasure and is highly motivated to learn movements such as jumping, skipping and running, using discovery and make-believe as aids to extrapolate their energy and activate their cognitive capacities.

The concrete operative period (7 to 12 years) involves construction games that are classified as a transition between symbolic and rule-based games. This stage also sees the development of rule-based games, where the child starts to develop a sociable construction of play through rules and activities where co-operation can be used as an educational element, which does not limit them from taking part in competitive activities, despite the fact that they are in dire need of interacting with other children in order to enter social reality.

In the formal operative stage (12 years upwards), the child begins to play by the rules, through very sociable practices such as sport, cultural competitions, excursions and other activities that allow interpersonal intelligence to develop.

We will focus more on symbolic and construction games in order to think about making activities and games aimed at psychomotricity, because we believe that in a later study, we will build new ways of teaching children with autism through Learning Mediation Scales (Annex 1), drawing sessions with the students and activities involving psychomotricity.

In order to place children in the context of stimulating psychomotor skills through games and play, we can use the following approximation of the facts to realise that well-designed programmed lessons that are adapted to the child's age can, through the manipulation of objects in their content, be a strong trigger for awakening the child's interest in the suggested games. According to Freire (1997, pg. 115): "In a school context, the game proposed as a way of teaching content to children (...) is not just any game, but a game transformed into a pedagogical instrument, a means of teaching".

Complementing the author's statement, we must interpret ways of playing the game in such a way as to stimulate the coordinative action of the body, to reach and foster the child's intelligence, also interpreting it as a pedagogical tool. Wouldn't psychomotricity be a way to build this?

Bearing in mind that play results from the expressiveness of the body and its possibility of use, using the body to enter through activities, involving psychomotricity,

6

in the child's cognitive stimulus, in addition to sticking to all this information in the elaboration of classes that provide through educational practices psychomotricity as an activation of thoughts and intellectual, physical and educational development, that is why we chose this science as a means of teaching and to elaborate a playful plan with the child interest of the autistic.

Psychomotricity has achieved a great deal in the area of inclusion. In fact, it has led educators' gaze from the assumption that students like to use their bodies to interact with people and objects, since this science deals with the study of human movement and everyone in their daily development uses it to socialise, learn and relate affectively. According to Fonseca (2008, p. 15) "Motricity thus simultaneously and sequentially becomes the first structure of relationship and co-relationship with the environment {...}". We can see that human movement is something spontaneous, where we discover our surroundings and interact with them through the possibilities of movement. This theme was conceived so that the integration between the AEE classroom and psychomotricity could be put into practice, propagating in the school's teaching practice the constant exercise of developing motor and psychological skills in students with autism, favouring dynamism so that, in their routine, they can, during the practice of activities, learn from playing, in a playful way to arouse interest in these activities. According to Fonseca (2008, pg. 266):

> Language is not limited to the auditory-verbal process. It internalises or incorporates countless tactile, kinaesthetic, proprioceptive, vestibular, postural, somatognostic, attentional and, of course, visual, visuomotor, etc. processes of great cognitive importance.

Routine and movement are part of the autistic child's daily life. It is interesting to realise that communication or the absence of verbal communication is a characteristic of ASD (Autism Spectrum Disorder) (SURIAN, 2010 pg. 10). Analysing this, we realise that the praxis of visual perceptual skills is useful for bringing verbal or non-verbal communication closer to the development of learning, using psychomotricity as a possible response to the learning process in students with autism.

7

To this end, we are thinking of developing these routine activities in a space to be built in the ESA classrooms, with objects that we will use in an organised way during the psychomotor activities developed.

With a view to building knowledge and enhancing the learning of autistic students through the development of activities, we hope that this development involving the study of psychomotor tasks with visuoperceptive skills can improve the specialised educational care plan, specifying through these activities a teaching routine for autistic students, favouring the conduct of this process as a theoretically based educational practice to provide a democratically inclusive school environment. We believe that the use of psychomotor activities involving repeated educational practices and organised routinely within two sessions of thirty minutes each, can encourage students with autism to practice executive functions, which are: "processes of control and coordination of the functioning of the cognitive system and encompass the ability to shift and maintain attention to pertinent information to complete a task, make plans{...}" (SURIAN, 2010 pg. 77) which in autism are so weakened because of the disorder. In this process of elaboration, we are thinking about school inclusion through this teaching strategy, respecting the skills and affect in the interaction with objects observed in children with ASD.

As part of the school inclusion process, we need students to stay in school and participate functionally. This requires a new outlook, new learning and teaching methods that correlate with the different school clientele.

CHAPTER 3

A BRIEF HISTORICAL ACCOUNT OF AEE AND INCLUSIVE EDUCATION

In the period before Christ, people with disabilities were abandoned and had two functions: to enrich the nobles by working or to take part in battles. As the vast majority of disabled people had difficulty performing these functions, they were discriminated against and left on the margins of society.

In the 12th century, during the Christian period, people began to look at disabled people as beings with souls, with looks of pity, but with the Protestant reformation, discrimination began again, and people with disabilities were labelled heretics and demonised.

In the 16th century, during the period of Protestantism, people with disabilities were chosen to pay for the sins of humanity. It wasn't until the 1940s, with the declaration of human rights (1948), that schools began to change their way of working to include all students.

According to Ropoli (2010, p. 8):

> Inclusive education sees the school as a place for everyone, in which students build knowledge according to their abilities, express their ideas freely, actively participate in teaching tasks and develop as citizens, regardless of their differences.

Reflecting from the perspective of inclusive mainstream schools, we have many steps to take with this statement. History, together with human rights, proposes that we expand the regular school to make it inclusive, but how to make this system work is up to us as professionals to rethink and build a school for everyone.

During the 1960s, some private institutions adhered to the declaration of human rights and began to welcome people with disabilities into their schools. During this period, philanthropic institutions were set up in Brazil to accommodate people with disabilities. From the perspective of philanthropy, we realise that: "in order to enhance specialised educational care we need all the school's actions to become a continuous movement of inclusion" Bedaque (2015, p. 22), in Brazil the APAE (Association of

Parents and Friends of the Exceptional) was created, with the purpose of inclusion and integration of the disabled. The role of inclusion is established in the regular school, the institution responsible for welcoming and developing educational practices for all. Later on, we'll look at an article in Resolution 04/2009 (which is attached), which explains the role of ESA rooms in Brazilian schools.

Figure 1 - Difference in paradigms

The 1990s were a decade of great importance for the inclusion of people with disabilities in our country. With the World Conference on Education for All, Brazil and the Ministry of Education published the Ten-Year Plan for Education for All for the period 1993-2003, drawn up in fulfilment of the Conference's resolutions. EDUCATION FOR ALL PROGRAMME (Universalisation of education).

Figure 2 - Inclusion flag

In 1990, the Jomtiem Declaration told us that: although the document highlights the rights of people with disabilities, it affirms their participation in the education system and addresses the need for schools to offer access, which for us means

10

democratising education and universalising it, making it available to everyone and ensuring that they stay in school.

The Salamanca Declaration (1994), which also took place in the 1990s, aimed to inform policies and guide governmental actions and other institutions towards their implementation on principles, policy and practice in Special Needs Education. The Inter-American Convention for the Elimination of All Forms of Discrimination against Persons with Disabilities was held in Guatemala in 1999.

Figure 3 - Salamanca Declaration

In Brazil, Article 58 of the LDBEN/1996 (National Education Guidelines and Basis Law) states that: "Special education, for the purposes of this law, is understood to be the type of school education offered preferentially in the regular school network, for students with disabilities, global development disorders and high abilities or giftedness." Under these terms of the law, the Brazilian state's role is to ensure that people with disabilities have access to and remain in mainstream education.

The UN (2006), for its part, drew up the Convention on the Rights of Persons with Disabilities, which states that people with disabilities are, first and foremost, people like any other, with a leading role, peculiarities, contradictions and singularities. This Convention was ratified by decree 186/2008, the MEC's National Special Education Policy (2008).

Finally, we have in history, specifically in Brazil, and in special education policies, the Berinice Piana Law of 28 December 2012, which establishes the National Policy for the Protection of the Rights of People with Autism Spectrum Disorders. In this extract, the Law tells us that:

> Art. 4 It is the duty of the state, the family, the school community and society to ensure the right of people with autism spectrum disorder to education, in an inclusive educational system, guaranteeing the transversality of special education from early childhood education to higher education.

Based on history, conventions, resolutions and laws, we have tried to introduce readers to how we arrived at the production of this care plan, based on the law and trying to integrate it with teaching through new ways of including innovative pedagogical practices in ESA classrooms. Article 9 of Resolution 04/2009 states that:

> Drawing up and implementing the ESA plan is the responsibility of the teachers who work in the multifunctional resource room or ESA centres, in conjunction with other sectoral health and social services, among others.

We understand that in this work we are trying to agree on the need to articulate a care plan based on the science of psychomotricity, so that we can innovate educational practices in ESA classrooms.

CHAPTER 4

METHODOLOGY

This study is qualitative in nature, based on bibliographical research, a construction/elaboration of psychomotor activities involving specifically perceptual-visual capacities to be carried out as a teaching practice in ESA classrooms, and the research is based on documentary and book analysis. Reading the work proposed by Falkenbach, Diesel and Oliveira (2010, p. 204), we noted that "The sessions are developed in a routine consisting of the entrance and exit rites and the moment of play". When drawing up this care plan, we will use the routine, the moment of entry and play as the basis for the proposed schedule of activities. This research will be carried out during sessions at the Marineide Pereira da Cunha Municipal School, located in the municipality of Mossoró - RN, with students with ASD (Autism Spectrum Disorder) in the early years of primary school as the population.

We relied on various authors, such as Fonseca, Falkenbach and Surian, as well as the books and bibliographies used in this specialisation in Specialised Educational Assistance. Below we describe the plan with the targeted activities involving psychomotor skills as teaching.

CHAPTER 5

RESULTS/DISCUSSION

SUGGESTED ROADMAP FOR THE SPECIALISED EDUCATIONAL CARE PLAN.

A. **Care plan:**

1- **Objective: To** develop visuoperceptive psychomotor skills in students with autism as a resource for learning.

2- Organisation of service:

Period: March to December

Frequency: Twice a week

Time: Thirty minutes

Composition of the service: ( ) Collective (x) Individual

Other: it can also be practised collectively.

3- Activities to be carried out in student care:

PSYCHOMOTOR ACTIVITIES INVOLVING VISUAL PERCEPTUAL SKILLS.

1-   Geometry matching activity, puzzle effect;

2- Activity of fitting coloured circles, each colour representing a number, from one to five (1- yellow; 2- green; 3- red; 4- blue *and 5* - black)

3- Activity of putting coloured balls into jars with the five vowels (A - Blue; E - Black; I - Green; O - Red; U- White)

4-Handle boxes of   various sizes, from DVDs to matchboxes and other box sizes;

5-Handle books of various sizes, comic books and magazines;

6-Put   each symbol in a box whose size matches that of the object. Example: put the EVA vowels in one box, the numbers in another and the geometric figures in another.

7-Remove   each symbol from the boxes and put them in a legible or understandable position;

8- Magic square   , use it to draw figures, lines and then ask the student to repeat the drawings;

9-Use   plain white sheets with dark backgrounds so that the student can follow the suggested drawings;

10-Moving around the designated area to carry out the tasks.

activities and observing the books, magazines and stories tactically explored during the lessons.

4-Selection of materials to be produced for the student: Recycled materials, alternative toys could be made as a suggestion.

5-Material suitability   : The material must be light, without any danger of hurting the student when it is thrown, as well as being suited to the student's interests, with favourite images and figures chosen by the students.

6-Selection   of materials and equipment that need to be purchased: Matching toys with geometric figures;

wooden toys attached to the EVA board; EVA vowels; drawing figures printed on the toys to stimulate play; magazines, comic books, books, boxes of various sizes;

7-Types   of partnerships needed to improve service and production of materials: Library teacher or any teacher with manual skills to make the material and guidance from the physical education teacher to organise and make the toys.

8-School professionals   who will receive guidance from the ESA teacher on the services and resources offered to the student:

(x)   EAL classroom teacher

(x)   Physical education teacher

( ) Classmates

(x)   Pedagogical Director

(x)   Pedagogical Team ( ) Other Which:

4- Evaluation of results

4- **Indication of recording methods: According to the** student's progress in fitting; learning numbers; colours; vowels; letters; images; visualisation and recognition of stories; drawings etc.
5- **Restructuring the plan**

Source: Bedaque (2015, p. 50 - 51)

This care plan was based on the study carried out in this research on visual perceptual activities. The plan is modelled on the one suggested by Bedaque.

For Getseman apud Fonseca (2015, p. 262) there is "the idea that perceptual-visual training promotes the potential for non-verbal and verbal learning", which made us realise how much visuoperceptual skills can favour the learning of children with autism, since verbal communication is frank and for SURIAN (2010, p. 13) "autism is characterised by a persistent lack of communication".

According to Frostig apud Fonseca (2015, p. 282)

> It is in the dialogue and interaction between visual information, auditory information and tactile-kinesthetic information that the child learns about objects and their respective structures, and articulates and dynamises the entire cognitive process, which in turn will allow the discovery of their attributes, properties and meanings.

We hope to be able to teach from the playful elaboration of play as a cognitive construction of executive functions that can, from recall and memory, favour the learning of children with autism. Within the activities suggested here, we have considered this kinaesthetic tactile action in activities 1, 2 and 3, attributing this kinaesthetic tactile development to what we call visual-motor coordination. Based on these activities, we can question and ask the student about "Spatial relations: a competence that consists of the ability to recognise and detect the position of spatial data in objects, figures, points, letters or numbers in relation to each other, in their relationship with the individual" (FONSECA, 2015, p. 285). The relationship between the student and their external environment is concrete in the activities proposed here. The repeated approximation of what is seen and what is done tactically can help the

16

student's learning process.

In Activities 4 and 5 we worked on the consistency of shapes from the book with boxes of different sizes. We also observed the intensity of the force involved in moving each object. According to Fonseca (2015, p. 284), the recognition of shapes "also occurs in the recognition of letters whose component strokes are confused". Using the student's predilections when making the material makes all the difference, as this student will remain in the classroom and in the teaching-learning process much more often.

During activities 6 and 7, in addition to the child being in an environment delimited by the colours of the figures, spatial position will be worked on by allowing these students to organise the area by placing each symbol worked on during the lesson inside a shoebox: the numbers will be in a box, the vowels and the geometric figures will also be in a box.

In activities 8 and 9 we developed the background figure as a means of teaching how to handle the pencil, to start writing using the material that helps us in the classroom.

To finalise the routine and to leave the place where we work on psychomotor skills, we situate the student in the place and space. Once again we look at the shapes of the books, magazines and comics used in class and move to another area of the classroom.

CHAPTER 6

FINAL CONSIDERATIONS

We hope to have contributed to an educational practice that, by elucidating the visual perceptual capacities of students with ASD, can help develop the inclusion routine in mainstream schools, taking into account these factors: the interest of students with ASD in activities (involving objects); their affective behaviour during the praxis; interaction with objects and the favouring of this practice as a stimulus for executive functions. We hope to develop these activities in the ESA classrooms. Observing the learning process as the product of all these factors, we designed these psychomotor activities with the organisation of routine in the classrooms of regular schools in mind.

We were able to come up with activities that involved perceptual-motor skills and thus achieved the expected results. To this end, we need to make this construction a reality by consolidating this practice in the schools' ESA rooms. We started from the need to promote inclusion in mainstream schools, favouring an educational practice that develops learning in students with autism spectrum disorders, to foster school inclusion, noting that "From the perspective of inclusive education, special education becomes part of the pedagogical proposal of the mainstream school{...}". BRASIL (2007). We propose to develop this care plan at the school based on this elaboration.

We hope that the possibilities of observation by the professionals involved in the learning of students with autism can be broadened and thus the construction of activities that arouse interest in ASD can emerge.

Braga Júnior; Belchior; Santos (2015, p.23):

> Generally speaking, the social integration of a person with autism spectrum disorder is not an easy process, as it involves the task of placing a person whose behaviour is strange and unfamiliar to most people in an unprepared social environment.

We would like this work to contribute to the school environment, and for us to be able to develop routines every day that contextualise the construction of being,

18

learning and living together for all students, for the school to be welcoming and overflowing with an inclusive environment that respects diversity and unites different ways of thinking. That students with special educational needs can be in the school environment and develop in their own way in and from school.

ANNEX I

ROUTINE FOR AUTISTIC PEOPLE: POSSIBILITIES OF ELABORATION THROUGH PICTORIAL COMMUNICATION SYMBOLS FAVOURING INCLUSION AT SCHOOL

Paula Gomes da Silva

PRESENTATION

This work was written to be presented at the IV SEADIS (UFERSA's Seminar on Affirmative Action, Diversity and Inclusion). In its preparation, we used the responses of the professionals involved in the school, who are directly responsible for planning lessons with the student, in joint action with the AEE (Specialised Educational Assistance).

Based on this, we will begin a study aimed at developing activities involving the science of psychomotricity so that, through this study, we can build a school environment full of possibilities for students with autism and other learners. According to Bedaque (2015, p 13): "Promoting a school for all, requires an understanding of a school that attends to, recognises and values differences in all moments of interaction and educational practices. "We think of a regular school that welcomes and provides professionals with continuing education, who are willing to use their knowledge to build an inclusive school.

In this paper, we will outline and describe the development of a research project and methodology, based on action research and interviews, we will transcribe the MAS

19

(Mediated Learning Scale) and methodologically use the Pictorial Communication Symbols (PECS) as a proposed activity. We used the bibliographical review and the MAS to delimit this expanded summary, and we also used articles to base ourselves theoretically and to construct the proposed activities. We hope that this work will enable the exercise of yet another method to be developed in the school environment in partnership with the pedagogical team and the ESA room.

1. Introduction

In this study, a routine was devised to enable an autistic nine-year-old student, enrolled in the 4th year of primary school in a school in the north-eastern region of Brazil, to learn. The Operationalised Version of the Scale for Evaluating the Mediated Learning Experience (EAM) (CUNHA, 2004; CUNHA; ENUMO; CANAL, 2006) to observe the reception of the educational practices of the Teacher; Intermediate Teacher and student, we think that from this work, an article related to educational practices, psychomotricity and autism will follow. "Autism Spectrum Disorders (ASD) are diagnosed in increasing numbers and also at an increasingly early age in Brazil" (MELLO, 2013, pg. 37). This reality instigates us to observe, research and deepen our knowledge of educational practices that can provide the integration of these students in schools. According to SURIAN (2010, pg. 10): "Autism is a neuropsychological development disorder that manifests itself through marked and persistent difficulties in social interaction, communication and in the repertoire of interests and activities", observing these characterisations of autism, we found a way in which the learning process at school could be developed from a routine based on the children's possible interests , thus favouring the student's social interaction by means of pictorial communication symbols (PCS) as an aid to this construction.

Within the process of school inclusion, we need students to remain in school and functionally participate in it, for this a new look is needed, a new learning and teaching methods that correlate the different school clientele, "special education directs its actions to meet the specificities of these students in the educational process and, within the scope of a broader performance in the school..." BRASIL (2008), within this inclusive context, reported in the national policy of special education from the perspective of inclusive education, the elaboration of routine must, in the analysis of this work, make it possible for this student to settle into the school scenario and integrate the routine activity with his special educational needs, thinking together with the classroom teacher and the intermediate teacher, how best to develop this conviviality in the teaching and learning process starting from an evaluation scale.

2. Methodology

The methodology involved the application of a questionnaire with the intermediate teacher and the classroom teacher, for the development and elaboration of the routine, analysed using the Operationalised Version of the Mediated Learning Experience Evaluation Scale (EAM) (CUNHA, 2004; CUNHA; ENUMO; CANAL, 2006) and the use of pictorial communication symbols in the construction and development of the routine.

The questionnaire contained five questions about ASD: questions about the student's interests; questions related to continuing education with teachers; and about assistive technology. An analysis was carried out with the class teacher and the intermediate teacher about the student, considering their mediation with the student, the results of which are represented in a graph in figure 1 according to the Mediated Learning Experience Rating Scale. "MLE is the main concept of the Mediated Learning Experience theory." (CUNHA; ENUMO and CANAL, 2006). Through the questionnaire, we sought to analyse the level of contingent responsiveness, affective involvement and change generated by this mediating process on a scale between 1 and 3. We assumed that the more the student is known, the more there will be affection and observation of the child, favouring the satisfactory development of the routine, as well as its elaboration.

We devised a routine in which we took into account the student's introduction to the school and their interaction with other colleagues in the classroom and outside it. The Pictorial Communication symbols are part of the routine, and we also use the intermediate teacher's speech, along with the symbols in figure 2, in order to favour the student's interaction with colleagues and professionals involved in the educational process, as well as directing him to use the toilet and integrating him into classroom activities, at snack time and break time. "[...] Assistive Technology is related to adaptive devices for people with disabilities with the aim of promoting greater independence to perform tasks that they were previously unable to perform [...]" (GONÇALVES; FURTADO, 2015, pg. 47), among the categories of assistive technology, Alternative Communication exists to provide students with special educational needs with a resource that favours communication, which can be built or obtained in the form of software, PCS and other categories.

3. Results

The results were drawn up as follows: we carried out a questionnaire and from the five questions, formulated about ASD; questions about the student's interests in activities; questions related to continuing education with teachers and about assistive technology, we analysed the answers and the degree of mediation between teachers and students according to the Mediated Learning Experience Scale (MLE), with the aim of better designing the routine based on the teachers' answers and their interaction with the child.

The Scale was of the utmost importance because it allowed us to observe the child's behaviour and language, so that we could study methods other than pictorial communication symbols (PC'S) that enable the teaching and learning process for autistic children.

Next, we'll look at the assistive technology of Pictorial Communication Symbols as a method that favours everyday living and we'll transcribe the routine to be followed. Remember that this planning and report, described in brief, was carried out with a specific student from the municipal school system.

4. Figures and Tables

FIGURE 1
Reference: CUNHA; ENUMO; CANAL, 2006

In FIGURE 1 - We realised that the intermediate teacher was able to develop a much better psychosocial relationship with his student than the classroom teacher, so we considered, based on the questionnaire, his answers to be much better than the classroom teacher and we achieved success with the student. As for changes, with the application of the questionnaire, the classroom teacher began to review his practices and turned his gaze to the student in order to research and interact with the ESA teacher and the intermediate teacher, bringing about a similar change in the student as a mediator of learning.

FIGURE 2

In FIGURE 2 - Contains the symbols whose routine was drawn up from them, the

23

step-by-step routine follows:

Step 1: We use all the symbols 1; 2; 3; 4; 5, so that as soon as the intermediate teacher arrives in the classroom he can talk to the student about the routine, he verbalises to the child what their day will be like by showing them the symbols;

Step 2: During the lesson, the teacher remains on symbol 3, exemplifying the reading and activities developed in class;

Step 3: Throughout the day, the intermediate teacher uses the 2 symbol to encourage the student to interact with their colleagues and other staff members.

Step 4: When the child needs to go to the toilet, use the symbol 1 to help them recognise the space where they need to go;

Step 5: During snack time, the teacher will show the symbol 5;

Step 6: During recess or in PE class, the student will be shown symbol 4, referring to playing with objects.

4. Conclusion

Thinking of the routine as the synchrony of the school project, this elaboration came about so that the mediation between teachers and autistic students could be effective, we realised that the questionnaire helped us a lot to build this awareness of an inclusive school, not only with students with special educational needs, but it also served to reprogramme the activities of the classroom teacher, "When we talk about school inclusion, the idea that comes to mind would be to simply put a child with Autism Spectrum Disorder in a mainstream school, expecting them to start imitating the other children [....]" (BRAGA JUNIOR; BELCHIOR e SANTOS, 2015, pg. 23). To this end, the routine proposal, as an analysed and generated response to the development of autistic students, makes it possible to respect differences and guides how we should proceed in order to enhance the student's abilities.

We hope to have achieved our goal by creating a routine that is part of the school setting and favours the teaching-learning process of students with special educational needs, providing the actors in this process (intermediate teacher and classroom teacher) with the tools to better understand and assess the development of these students.

6. Keywords: Routine; Autism; Assistive Technology

ANNEX II

SCHOOL PHYSICAL EDUCATION, DIVERSITY AND INCLUSION: PERSPECTIVES ON CLASSES WITH AUTISTIC PEOPLE

Paula Gomes da Silva

SUMMARY

This paper reports on the experience of recreational classes with an autistic student, a 2nd year B student in primary school, in a school in the north-eastern region of Brazil. It was carried out with a view to some perspectives of interaction and school coexistence based on an inclusive methodology, which makes it possible to respect the diversities and differences leveraged in the discourse of a common and inclusive school. Through the report of experiences in classes with an autistic student in a mainstream school, based on a constructivist approach mediated by the Physical Education teacher from a perspective of interaction, inclusion and play, this article makes it possible, in the methodological description, to reflect on respect and stimulation of the body, within the expectations of a school for all.

Key words: Inclusion; Lessons and games.

1- INTRODUCTION

Thinking of a school for all, which would enable the inclusion of children with Autism within the parameters of respect for diversity and differences, we formulated Physical Education classes that would awaken in the students, through Play, the inclusion of everyone in the 2nd year B class, of this given school.

25

The lessons were based on themes generated by the student and developed using a constructivist approach, mediated by the Physical Education teacher, with cirandas de roda as part of the content, in order to provide inclusion through play, making it possible for all the students to interact.

Thinking of an inclusive school where "inclusion breaks with the paradigm that sustains the conservatism of schools, challenging educational systems in their foundations." Ropoli (2010, p.7), we decided to use corporeality to make this practice possible from the perspective of inclusion.

2- Justification

Realising the need for teachers to think about inclusion in this school as a source of research and student development, this work was written with the aim of reporting on the classes designed to adapt and encourage interaction between the children, respecting and observing the diversity of each one. The physical education teacher was given the task of planning recreational and inclusive lessons.

Body practices for interaction are extremely important, because "bodily insufficiencies, in addition to modifying the human being's relationship with the world, are also very important".

world manifest themselves in differentiated behaviour in relationships with people" Falkenbach (2010). The students' corporeality was observed and fostered in the search for affective development and interaction between everyone. Playing favoured bodily activities and experiences in the body, based on the playful traits that stimulate children's doing. According to Freire (1997, pg. 85): "Among the pedagogical resources that physical education uses in its task of teaching, there is a particular one, which are bodily activities that come from the child's culture". This observation is significant for this work, as we believe that, based on the child's interest in corporeality, we have developed circle games and described them here in this report.

Thinking about physical education classes that stimulate thinking in children's phases by interacting "the plane of motor operations and the plane of mental representations" Fonseca (1999, p.39), summarises well classes codified under a look focused on movement, corporeality, as a cognitive stimulator, making it possible through planned activities not to dissociate body and mind in teaching, thus making the body an instrument of great influence for the acquisition of knowledge in childhood and inclusion in school.

3- PROBLEM

Designing lessons with students with autism from an inclusive perspective in an attempt to promote interaction, knowledge of the body and play. Looking for relationships that, according to Oliveira (2006), are realised through corporeality, which can only be understood from a perspective of totality. These classes were developed through activities that involved cirandas and made it possible to recognise the body through play and interaction with others, this body being seen and understood as a whole, made up of all the students.

4- THEORETICAL BACKGROUND

With interaction activities, knowledge of the body and singing toys in constructivist classes as a milestone, we used some books as a basis to respect the diversity and differences of each student and to promote inclusion. Honora (2003) explains the varieties of disabilities through the ciranda of inclusion: "We must bear in mind that no human being is the same as another. The same is true of people with disabilities, none is the same as another, what we must remember is that individual particularities must be taken into account". With this in mind, a study was carried out on autism, which, according to Surian (2014), "manifests itself fundamentally and concerns the lack of age-appropriate social interaction". With all the observation of the behavioural signs emitted by the student and thinking about the themes generated by her, the classes were developed from a constructivist approach, which, for Darido (2000), has as its purpose, "The construction of knowledge". This construction was mediated by the teacher and experienced by all the students in the school's 2nd year of primary school. All these ideas made it possible to start thinking about inclusion in

Physical Education classes because, according to Silva and Costa (2015), "When we oppose a school that segregates, it is necessary to think about a school structure that does not allow marginalisation either". Thus, the classes were consolidated with everyone's participation, fulfilling the role of an inclusive common school. This discourse does not finalise the future work to be done, nor does it end here, but only nurtures new perspectives in Physical Education classes for the inclusion of autistic people.

5- METHODOLOGY

The classes are given two days a week, each session lasting fifty minutes, by the Physical Education professional. The 2nd year B students take part as a whole, and the pupil is part of this body. The classes are mediated by the teacher using a constructivist approach, with content filled with popular games, ciranda de roda, and the most diverse variations of singing toys. The lessons are based on observation of the autistic student.

We used the child's cognitive development as a parameter for the school years, assuming that they would be taught within the age range suggested by the school. It is worth emphasising that this age is not stereotyped, and that there may be older or younger children in the classroom. We also noted that the student has special educational needs, due to the global development disorder that is characteristic of each autistic individual, but through the methodological suggestions, the teaching-learning situations are adaptable to the adverse conditions in the classroom - it is a matter of observing the social, cultural and economic context experienced by the students, and that during the development of the content, they must have their co-participation for better consolidation of knowledge.

6- DEVELOPMENT WITH THE RESULTS

Plans are drawn up with the themes generated by the student in mind, from an inclusive perspective. The games are programmed and problematised with the content of popular games, Cirandas de Roda, activities that favour the interaction of each person. In terms of knowledge about the body, individual and collective observation of the space each person occupies, the intensity of touching the other, shaking hands, makes the body known, situated in time, space and coexistence with the other, enabling interaction, respect and affection.

According to Oliveira (2006): "Bodily practices are elusive, difficult to record and apprehend, impossible to reduce to any discursive form other than the practices themselves in their moment of realisation," and it was with this record of corporeality in mind that we described this report. Thinking about creative development and building together with the student, based on her motivations, the bodily practice of all the school's students.

7- CONCLUSION

At the end of the class period, we realised that the students had experienced the activities intensely and that the interaction, the knowledge of the body and the problematisations generated from the ciranda de roda made it possible to respect diversity and differences, making them understand that coexistence through play is possible, broadening the perspectives of inclusion. This work has only generated the beginning, a starting point from the point of view of the various perspectives that exist in classes with autistic children. Looking to creativity, studies and the school's teaching staff for classroom possibilities is part of the thinking behind an inclusive school. We have a lot to do to provide our students with a school for everyone.

ANNEX III

MINISTRY OF EDUCATION NATIONAL EDUCATION COUNCIL CHAMBER OF BASIC EDUCATION RESOLUTION NO. 4, OF 2 OCTOBER 2009 (*)

> Establishes Operational Guidelines for Specialised Educational Assistance in Basic Education, Special Education modality.

The President of the Basic Education Chamber of the National Education Council, in the use of his legal attributions, in accordance with the provisions of Article

9(c) of Law No. 4.024/1961, as amended by Law No. 9.131/1995, as well as Article 90, Paragraph 1 of Article 8 and Paragraph 1 of Article 9 of Law No. 9.394/1996, considering the Federal Constitution of 1988; Law No. 10.098/2000; Law No. 10.436/2002; Law No. 11.494/2007; Decree No. 3.956/2001; Decree No. 5.296/2004; Decree No. 5.626/2005; Decree No. 6.253/2007; Decree No. 6.571/2008; and Legislative Decree No. 186/2008, and on the basis of CNE/CEB Opinion No. 13/2009, ratified by Order of the Minister of State for Education, published in the Official Gazette of 24 September 2009, resolves:

Art. 1 In order to implement Decree No. 6.571/2008, education systems must enrol students with disabilities, global developmental disorders and high abilities in ordinary regular education classes and in Specialised Educational Assistance (AEE), offered in multifunctional resource rooms or in Specialised Educational Assistance centres in the public network or in non-profit community, confessional or philanthropic institutions.

Art. 2 AEE's function is to complement or supplement the student's education by providing services, accessibility resources and strategies that eliminate barriers to their full participation in society and the development of their learning.

Sole Paragraph. For the purposes of these Guidelines, accessibility resources in education are considered to be those that ensure conditions of access to the curriculum for students with disabilities or reduced mobility, promoting the use of teaching and learning materials, spaces, furniture and equipment, communication and information systems, transport and other services.

Art. 3 Special Education takes place at all levels, stages and modalities of education, with Special Education as an integral part of the educational process.

Art. 4 For the purposes of these Guidelines, the target audience for ESA is considered to be:

I - Students with disabilities: those who have long-term physical, intellectual, mental or sensory impairments.

31

II - Students with global developmental disorders: those who present alterations in neuropsychomotor development, impairment in social relationships, communication or motor stereotypes. This definition includes students with classic autism, Asperger's syndrome, Rett's syndrome, childhood disintegrative disorder (psychoses) and invasive disorders without other specification.

III - Students with high abilities/gifted: those who show high potential and great involvement in the areas of human knowledge, isolated or combined: intellectual, leadership, psychomotor, arts and creativity.

(*) Resolution CNE/CEB 4/2009. Federal Official Gazette, Brasília, 5 October 2009, Section 1, p. 17.

Art. 5 AEE is carried out, as a priority, in the multifunctional resource room of the school itself or in another regular education school, in the reverse shift of schooling, and is not a substitute for ordinary classes, and can also be carried out in a Specialised Educational Care centre of the public network or of non-profit community, confessional or philanthropic institutions, in agreement with the Department of Education or equivalent body of the States, Federal District or Municipalities.

Art. 6 In cases of Specialised Educational Assistance in a hospital or home environment, students will be offered complementary or supplementary Special Education by the respective education system.

Art. 7 Students with high abilities/giftedness will have their curriculum enrichment activities developed within the framework of regular public schools in interface with activity centres for high abilities/giftedness and with higher education institutions and institutes aimed at developing and promoting research, the arts and sports.

Art. 8 Students enrolled in ordinary public school classes who are concurrently enrolled in AEE will be double-counted under FUNDEB, in accordance with Decree 6.571/2008.

Sole Paragraph. Funding for ESA enrolment is conditional on enrolment in regular public school education, as recorded in the School Census/MEC/INEP for the previous year:

a) enrolment in the same public school's ordinary classroom and multifunctional resource room;

b) enrolment in a regular classroom and in a multifunctional resource room in another public school;

c) enrolment in a regular classroom and in a Specialised Educational Care centre at a public special education institution;

d) enrolment in an ordinary classroom and in a Specialised Educational Care centre at non-profit community, denominational or philanthropic Special Education institutions.

Art. 9 The preparation and implementation of the ESA plan is the responsibility of the teachers who work in the multifunctional resource room or ESA centres, in conjunction with the other regular education teachers, with the participation of families and in interface with the other sectoral services of health, social assistance, among others necessary for the service.

Art. 10: The pedagogical project of the regular school must institutionalise the provision of ESL, including in its organisation:

I - multifunctional resource room: physical space, furniture, teaching materials, pedagogical and accessibility resources and specific equipment;

II - enrolment in the EEA of students enrolled in regular education at the school itself or at another school;

III   - student attendance schedule;

IV - ESA plan: identification of the students' specific educational needs, definition of the necessary resources and the activities to be developed;

V   - teachers for teaching in the EEA;

VI - other education professionals: translators and interpreters of Brazilian Sign

Language, interpreter-guides and others who provide support, especially for feeding, hygiene and mobility activities;

VII - support networks within the scope of professional work, training, research development, access to resources, services and equipment, among others, that maximise ESA.

Sole Paragraph. The professionals referred to in item VI work with students who are the target audience for Special Education in all the school activities in which they are needed.

Art. 11: The ESA proposal, set out in the pedagogical project of the public or private non-profit Specialised Educational Care centre, which has signed an agreement for this purpose, must be approved by the respective Department of Education or equivalent body, taking into account the organisation set out in article 10 of this Resolution. Sole Paragraph. Specialised Educational Care centres must comply with the legal requirements established by the Education Council of the respective education system, as regards their accreditation, operating authorisation and organisation, in line with the guidelines set out in these Operational Guidelines.

Art. 12: In order to work in AEE, teachers must have initial training that qualifies them to teach and specific training for Special Education.

Art. 13: The duties of the Specialised Educational Assistance teacher are:

I - identifying, designing, producing and organising services, pedagogical resources, accessibility and strategies that take into account the specific needs of students targeted by Special Education;

II - drawing up and implementing a Specialised Educational Care plan, assessing the functionality and applicability of teaching and accessibility resources;

III - organising the type and number of services provided to students in the multifunctional resource room;

IV - monitor the functionality and applicability of pedagogical and accessibility resources in the regular classroom, as well as in other school environments;

34

V - establish partnerships with cross-sectoral areas to draw up strategies and provide accessibility resources;

VI - advising teachers and families on the pedagogical and accessibility resources used by the student;

VII - teaching and using assistive technology in order to increase students' functional abilities, promoting autonomy and participation;

VIII - liaise with teachers in the ordinary classroom to provide services, pedagogical and accessibility resources and strategies that promote students' participation in school activities.

IX t. 14. This Resolution will come into force on the date of its publication, revoking any provisions to the contrary.

CESAR CALLEGARI

BIBLIOGRAPHICAL REFERENCES

BEDAQUE, S. A. **Specialised educational assistance**. Mossoró: EDUFERSA, 2015. 68p.

BRAZIL. Ministry of Education. Special Education Secretariat. **National Policy for Special Education from the Perspective of Inclusive Education**. Brasília: MEC, 2008a. Available at:
<http://peei.mec.gov.br/arquivos/politica_nacional_educacao_especial.pdf>.
Accessed on 12 May 2017.

_____. National Education Council. Chamber of Basic Education. **Resolution No. 4**, of 2 September 2009.

. Law No. 9394 of 20 December 1996. **LDBEN.** Establishes the Guidelines and Bases of National Education. Federal Official Gazette. Brasília, n°248, 1996.

. Law No. 12.764, of 27 December 2012. Establishes the National Policy for the Protection of the Rights of People with Autism Spectrum Disorders. Federal Official Gazette. Brasília, DF, 28 Dec. 2012.

_____. Ministry of Education. Secretariat for Special Education. **National Policy for Special Education from the Perspective of Inclusive Education**, 2008.

BRAGA JÚNIOR, F. V.; BELCHIOR, M. S.; SANTOS, S. T. **Global Development Disorders and High Abilities/Gifted.** Mossoró: EDUFERSA, 2015. 47p.

CHICON, José Francisco. **Game Pedagogical Mediation and Inclusion**. São Paulo: Fontoura, 2010.

CUNHA, A. C. B; ENUMO, S. R. F.; CANAL, C. P. P. **Operationalisation of a scale to analyse maternal mediation patterns: a study with visually impaired mother-child dyads**. Revista Brasileira de Educação Especial, Marilia, v.12, n.3, p.393-412, 2006.

CUNHA, Ana C. B.; FARIAS, Iara M.; MARANHÃO, Renata V. A. **Teacher-student interaction with autism in the context of inclusive education: analysis of the teacher's mediation pattern based on the** mediated learning experience **theory**. Rev. Bras. Ed. Esp., Marília-SP, v.14, n.3, p.365-384, Sep./Dec. 2008.

DARIDO, Suraya. **Physical Education at School: Issues and Reflections**. Guanabara, 2000.

FALKENBACH, A. P.; DIESEL, D.; OLIVEIRA, L. C. The play of autistic children in relational psychomotricity sessions. In: **Rev. Brasileira de ciências do esporte**. Campinas, v.31, p. 203-214. Jan. 2010.

FONSECA, Denise Grosso. *Physical Education: into and beyond movement.* Porto

Alegre: Mediação, 1999.

FONSECA, V. **Psychomotor development and learning**. Porto Alegre: Artmed, 2008. 577 p.

FREIRE, P. **Pedagogia da autonomia: saberes necessárias à prática educativa**. São Paulo

Paulo: Paz e Terra, 1996, 141p.

FREIRE, João Batista. **Full body education: Theory and practice of physical education**. São Paulo: Scipione, 1997.

GONÇAVES, M. J.; FURTADO, U. M. **Distance Education and Assistive Technology**. Mossoró: EDUFERSA, 2015. 72p.

HONORA, Márcia; FRIZANCO, Mary Lopes Esteves. **Ciranda da Inclusão: Clarifying disabilities**. São Paulo: Ciranda Cultural

KLEIN, Rejane Ramos; HATTGE, Morgana Domênica (eds.). **School Inclusion: Implications for the curriculum**. São Paulo: Paulinas, 2010.

MELLO, A. M. et al. **Portraits of autism in Brazil**. São Paulo: Gráfica da AMA, 2013.106p. (AMA - Associação de amigos do autista).

OLIVEIRA, Marcus Aurélio Taborda(org.). **Educação do corpo na escola brasileira**. Campinas, SP: Autores Associados, 2006.

ROPOLI, Edilene Aparecida. **Special education from the perspective of school inclusion: the inclusive ordinary school**. Brasília: Ministry of Education, Department of Special Education; Fortaleza: Federal University of Ceará.

SILVA, Aída Maria Monteiro; COSTA, Valdelúcia Alves da Costa (eds.). **Inclusive Education and Human Rights: contemporary perspectives**. São Paulo: Cortez, 2015.

SURIAN, Luca. **Autism: essential information for family members, educators and health professionals**. São Paulo: Paulinas, 2010.